"Man is the cruelest of all animals"
Friedrich Nietzsche (1)

"Humans and non-humans are animals. All deserve an equal right to be treated with dignity and respect. One species has no right to rule over another in any manner such as slavery or determining the other's fate as with death. Until humanity as a whole realizes this, no peace will ever be available"
Opal Dockery

ABOUT THE AUTHOR

Opal Dockery is an award-winning actress, writer, poet and speaker. As an actress, her films have screened at over 500 film festivals worldwide. A former burlesque dancer for over 20 years, she is the author of many books, including the inspirational autobiography THOUGHTS OF A STRIPPER: A Mother's Story. Opal was recently inducted in the Burlesque Hall of Fame. Ms. Dockery has a Bachelor's Degree in Psychology and a Master's Degree in Criminal Justice. She has been a vegan for over 50 years, and is an animal rights activist.

Find the library of books by Opal Dockery at:

https://www.lulu.com/spotlight/dixiepublishing

EMPATHY

By

OPAL DOCKERY

Empathy
By Opal Dockery
Copyright @ 2021 by
Dixie Publishing
First Printing 2021

Jack Truman Productions
aka Dixie Publishing
Company
P.O. Box 364
Lamar, Missouri 64759

Website:
http://lulu.com/spotlight/dixiepublishing

ISBN: 978-1-257-08077-9

Printed in the United
States of America

EMPATHY, which is the ability to step into the shoes of another living being, aiming to understand their feelings and perspectives, and to use that understanding to guide one's actions, is absent regarding those oppressed by humans – the animals (non-humans) (2).

The Buddha said, "All beings tremble before violence. All fear death. All love life. See yourself in others. Then whom can you hurt?" (55)

LOOK INTO MY EYES
By Opal Dockery

Look into my eyes
And you will realize
How I am like you
With Feelings, Spirit, and a Soul,
too.

Look into my eyes
And you will be surprised
That you can be my friend
Time and time again.

Look into my eyes
And you will see the size
Of all the pain
That still remains.

Look into my eyes
And tell me all the whys
That your race kills mine
Why can you not be kind?

Look into my eyes
And you will see the cries
Of all the suffering I endure
Is there not a cure?

Look into my eyes
And finalize your thoughts
As you see the reflection of
yourself.

I want to realize brotherhood or identity, not merely with the beings called human, but I want to realize identity with all life, even with such things that crawl on the earth."
Mahatma Gandhi (18)

A HUNTER'S POEM
By Lemuel T. Ward

A hunter shot at a flock of geese
That flew within his reach.

Two were stopped in their rapid
flight
And fell on the sandy beach.

The male bird lay at the water's
edge

And just before he died

He faintly called to his wounded
mate
And she dragged herself to his
side.

She beat her head and crooned to
him
In a way distressed
and wild
Caressing her one and only mate
As a mother would a child.

Then covering him with her
broken wing
And gasping with falling breath
She laid her head against his
Breast
A feeble honk ... then death.

This story is true though crudely
told.
I was the man in this case.

I stood knee-deep in snow and
cold
And the hot tears burned my
face.

I buried the birds in the sand
where they lay
Wrapped in my hunting coat.

And I threw my gun and belt in
the bay
When I crossed in the open boat.

Hunters will call me a right poor
sport
And scoff at the thing I did.
But that day something broke in
my heart
And shoot again? God forbid!
(3)

"When I was twelve, I went hunting with my father and we shot a bird. He was laying there and something struck me. Why do we call this fun to kill this creature who was as happy as I was when I woke up this morning?"
Marv Levy (18)

SPECIAL MESSAGE FROM THE AUTHOR

Many times people ask me, "Well, if animals are not here for us to eat, then why are they here?" Before we ask this question, we need to ask the question that civilization has been asking since the beginning of time - "Why are we here?"

I make a special plea to all humanity to please examine your **Heart** and **Soul** and then decide if the **PAIN** that is inflicted on the animals (non-humans) is worth the exploitation we constantly inflict on them. If we care about the animals (non-humans), we must remember that they have feelings, too. We must allow them to be our friends rather than our meals.

Take the meat off your breath and the dead animal (non-human) skin off your back to display your <u>EMPATHY</u> for animals (non-humans).

I sincerely hope that someday soon people will know it is wrong to exploit animals (non-humans). We must realize that they have their own separate cultures from us and respect them for their own unique species.

It is my hope that this book will serve as a purpose to

humanity by realizing that
EMPATHY must be exercised
in our society regarding the
treatment of animals
(non-humans) by displaying
evidence that they possess
emotions comparable to humans.

Let us all join in a concerted
effort to practice **EMPATHY**
regarding other living, feeling,
sentient beings by realizing they
possess feelings and want to live
in peace just as we do. We must
be their protectors and friends by
reaching a higher level of
existence!

**"In all the confines of the
human mind, we explore
the corridors as they
open, offering an
excellent opportunity for**

us to express and prove our worth as human beings by acknowledging the fact that animals possess emotions comparable to humans which should result in a display of human EMPATHY."
Opal Dockery

SPECIAL THANKS

I want to thank my son, Jack
Truman, for all the intense work
he performs for me regarding ALL
the books I have written and will
write. I am assured of having
them published due to his untiring
dedication of the technical aspects
regarding my writing projects as
well as his confidence in my
abilities. None of my work would
ever be published if not for his
untiring dedication as well as the
support he unselfishly gives me.
Thank you, my son. I love you.

DEDICATION

I dedicate this book as a contribution to all the countless millions and millions of animals (non-humans) who constantly experience daily unending suffering forced upon them with no hope in sight from generation to generation as a result of the lack of **EMPATHY** which is consistently practiced by the uncaring, selfish society of humans who utilize such animals (non-humans) for whatever they decide and turn a blind eye to their feelings and emotions of **PAIN**, suffering, and sadness.

HYPOTHESIS

Since animals (non-humans) are comparable to humans physically, then they are comparable to humans emotionally; therefore **EMPATHY** toward animals (non-humans) must be incorporated into the society of the human race.

STATEMENT OF PURPOSE

It is imperative that society break **'The Bonds Of Ignorance'** by climbing from **'The Depths Of Such Ignorance'** when totally disregarding failure to acknowledge the fact that animals (non-humans) possess feelings and emotions which are comparable to humans and realizing that it is vitally important to consistently exercise **<u>EMPATHY</u>** toward all animals (non-humans) by not killing them for any reason except in the case of self defense.

<u>ABSTRACT</u>

The purpose of this research is to enlighten the minds of humans to the fact that animals (non-humans) experience emotions comparable to humans and should be regarded with respect and not killed except in the case of self-defense. (6) This applies to all animals (non-humans) rather than just the ones which the human race decides should live or die such as giving preference to pets as well as endangered species over others like farm animals (non-humans) that suffer needlessly.

It is quite obvious by common sense observation as well as scientifically proven facts that animals (non-humans) are comparable to humans in most aspects of physiology and physically (8) which reflects feelings and emotions facilitated by the brain. The brain is necessary for all feeling and emotions in humans as well as animals (non-humans). Since this is a valid truth, then it is quite reasonable that the brains of animals (non-humans) are comparable to humans due to the fact that the brain is a physical part of the human and as well as the animal (non-human) body.

So why is it necessary to prove that animals (non-humans)

possess feelings and emotions; since it is quite obvious due to observation that this is true? It is a good idea to leave our comfort zones and to grow, in order to expand our horizons as we work to replace cruelty with

EMPATHY as well as compassion and dig deeply into our hearts.

People want to be good; so they make laws regarding the killing of animals (non-humans). Why is it so important to treat animals (non-humans) humanely if they have no feelings or emotions? It is acceptable to kill them as long as you do it humanely. What is so humane about killing? Animals (non-humans) deserve more, and we can always do better. (5)

Again, if animals (non-humans) have no emotions,

then why are there so many Statutes regarding animal (non-human) cruelty? One might wonder why states have animal (non-human) cruelty Statutes if killing animals (non-humans) is acceptable. (10) These rules and regulations are meaningless if animals' (non-humans') feelings do not matter. On one hand society recognizes that animals (non-humans) can feel **PAIN** by criminalizing animal (non-human) cruelty, and yet on the other hand, it is far from clear whether they truly believe that animals (non-humans) feel in a meaningful sense. (67)

Due to the fact that the legal system will not design legislation to protect animals (non-humans) and discontinue the **PAIN** that society inflicts on them, the exploitation of animals (non-humans) can only be stopped by humans joining together in a concerted effort to exercise **EMPATHY** to the fullest extent possible.

In mankind's quest for survival at the expense of the animals (non-humans), another survival is realized, **'Survival Of The Mind'**. It is imperative to incorporate **EMPATHY** into our dealings regarding animals (non-humans). Their suffering has been accepted far too long.

"The atrocities of against animals are horrendous. I am sorry for all the PAIN and suffering the animals must endure. I am sorry for all the ignorance which is portrayed in our society." Opal Dockery

INTRODUCTION

The purpose of this contribution
is an attempt to display the fact
that animals (non-humans)
experience emotions comparable
to humans. It is quite evident
they are similar to humans
physically which is proven
through observation. They
possess the same five senses as
humans. Their bodily functions
and physical activities are similar
such as Breathing, Eating,
Sleeping, Yawning, Defecating,
and Procreation. Based on these
facts alone, it is logical to
conclude that they are capable of
possessing emotions comparable
to humans. Since this is true,
humanity must exercise
EMPATHY and immediately
discontinue the vile acceptable
killings of animals (non-humans)

in all instances except in cases of self defense. Society is extremely barbaric as well as hypocritical in this regard due to the fact that it decides which animals (non-humans) are to be kept safe and secure, while blatantly disregarding the feelings and emotions of others who are consistently utilized for their own ignorant, selfish benefit such as Eating, Clothing, Sporting, and Experimentation.

"There are viable (and usually better) alternatives to the use of animals for food, sport, clothing, and experimentation. I beg you to discontinue any

actions that might cause or condone animal torture, abuse, or destruction." Moby (18)

Pets are precious to their owners, and in many cases, considered family members. One can be prosecuted for being cruel and killing some animals (non-humans) such as a dog or cat, even if they are strays. Protests are formed against killing animals (non-humans) that are used to produce fur. Endangered species are protected to prevent their becoming extent. But the feelings and emotions of the vast amount of others, such as farm animals (non-humans), are not considered as a result of the general public selfishly deciding which species should live or die.

Such ignorance is due to the low moral degree of humanity. (69)

"If he be really and seriously seeking to live a good life, the first thing from which he will abstain will always be the use of animal food, because...its use is simply immoral, as it involves the performance of an act which is contrary to the moral feeling, killing." Leo Tolstoy (18)

Legalized murder is extremely predominate in our 'so-called' compassionate, civilized world. The human species must elevate itself from **'The Depths Of**

Ignorance' by realizing the immediate, urgent need to exercise **<u>EMPATHY</u>** for all animals (non-humans) who are suffering as a result of humanity's Greed, Gluttonous, and Ignorance. If one loves animals (non-humans) how can he eat them? (5)

"Animals are my friends. I don't eat my friends." George Bernard Shaw (18)

I am saddened with the fact that the majority of cultures are quite conscious that animals (non-humans) are tortured and experience unnecessary **PAIN** when killed which people, unfeelingly, choose to ignore while promoting the legalized murder of such animals (non-humans) for their own ignorant selfish desires and benefit. This ignorant attitude is well accepted and woven so tightly into society worldwide that humanity, as a whole, has no **<u>EMPATHY</u>** for the exploited animals (non-humans) in this regard.

"Flesh eating is unprovoked murder." Benjamin Franklin. (18)

I feel especially sad regarding the plight of farm and factory housed animals (non-humans) due to the fact that humankind considers them only a product to utilize in whatever manner desired. These unfortunate animals (non-humans) are the ones most abused and exploited by society which includes the humiliating process of breeding which is beyond the consideration of being putrid.

In slaughterhouses, cows and pigs 'have' been observed to cry. **Such was seen of a pregnant cow who cried and kneeled at the slaughterhouse, begging for her life. (54)**

"The very people who shudder over the cruelty of the hunter are apt to forget that slaughter, in the grimmest sense of the word, is a process they entrust daily to the

**butcher; and that
unlike the game of the
forest, even the dumbest
creatures of the
slaughterhouse know
what is in store for
them."
Lewis Mumford (18)**

Total disregard for the
feelings of such unfortunate
animals (non-humans) is
displayed by society and the laws
which allows disgraceful horrid
actions such as eating meat and
eggs as well as wearing leather
while collaborating in the
appallingly cruel conditions under
which, in too many cases, those
goods are produced which
involves the torture of animals
(non-humans) such as calves,

chickens, and pigs. (10) "Isn't that little calf cute?" "See how it cuddles next to its mother?" "Aren't those little pigs sweet?" "They are so tiny and cute as they nurse their mother." "Oh! What darling baby chicks!" It is beyond my comprehension how the same people who make such comments display hypocrisy by their total disregard for the feelings of these animals (non-humans) based on their actions of eating hamburgers, pork chops, eggs, and chicken as well as wearing leather.

"But for the sake of some little mouthful of flesh we deprive a Soul of the sun and light, and of that proportion of life and

time it had been born into the world to enjoy."
Lucius Mestrius Plutarch (50)

Such animals (non-humans) are at the complete mercy of humans who decide to kill and use them for their own selfish convenience. There is no consideration for their feelings and emotions which are equally important as the animals (non-humans) who are consistently protected and treated with dignity as well as respect. It is unbelievable that such atrocious, hypocritical, uncaring actions exist in our so-called 'civilized' society.

"Let us taste 'The Sweet Meat Of Life' rather

than the flesh of
animals." Opal Dockery

Everyone in the world should
be required, at least, one time in
their life to visit a slaughterhouse.
Whoever can accept the slaughter
of these innocent animals
(non-humans) without any guilt
after witnessing such, is so far
saturated with ignorance and most
assuredly incapable of ever
reaching the **'ELEVATION
Of EMPATHY'** regarding
the consistent abuse of such
animals (non-humans).

**"I believe that an
animal's revenge lies
within each meateater's
body and mind due to the
unhealthy effects on the**

human body that meat eating causes as well as the moral issue."
Opal Dockery

It is of vital importance that **EMPATHY** toward all animals (non-humans) be incorporated into the society of the human race. Silence in this area has been predominate far too long.

Let us remember the term, Evolution. **'The Evolution Of The Mind'** will never be obtained until we reach the level of **EMPATHY** for all animals (non-humans). We must rise above the **'Stagnation'** of the ones who insist on the slaughter of animals (non-humans) for their putrid, selfish desires.

"I have no doubt that it is a part of destiny of the human race, in its gradual improvement, to leave off eating animals, as surely as the savage tribes have left off eating each other when they came into contact with the more civilized." *Walden, 1854* **Henry David Thoreau (18)**

We, as a human race, have evolved in many ways that surpass the caveman days. Why not rise above the unending slaughter and torment of animals (non-humans)? It is unnecessary to continue such uncaring acceptable practices. We are no longer cavemen and have found

ways to survive quite well
without killing animals
(non-humans) such as
manufacturing clothes as well as
healthy ways to eat in order to
save their lives from unnecessary
pain, torture, and death.

**"There will come a
time...when civilized
people will look back in
horror on our generation
and the ones that
preceded it: the idea that
we should eat other living
things running around
on four legs, that we
should raise them just for
the purpose of killing
them! The people of the
future will say, 'meat
eaters!' in disgust and**

**regard us in the same
way we regard cannibals
and cannibalism."
Dennis Weaver (18)**

It is my desire that this book
will raise awareness to the fact
that all animals (non-humans)
experience emotions comparable
to humans and should be treated
with the dignity and respect
which every living, feeling being
deserves. It is imperative that we
immediately break **'The Bonds
Of Ignorance'** that have kept us
trapped for much too long by
eliminating our uncaring, barbaric
actions. The **PAIN** and
suffering caused by our ignorant
greed and gluttonous must cease.

**"Truly man is the king of
beasts, for his brutality**

exceeds theirs. We live
by the death of others.
We are burial places!"
Leonardo Da Vinci (18)

It is past time for us to unite as a
civilized, caring society and
exercise **EMPATHY**
regarding the feelings of all
animals (non-humans) to the
fullest extent.

THE TIME IS NOW!!!!

"Journey into the depths
of your own personal
thoughts with the
accompaniment of
intensely deep
introspection regarding
your final decision."
Opal Dockery

"Be ashamed to die until you have won some victory for humanity."
Horace Mann (81)

The following research I offer is a contribution I make to the World. I hope that it will prove to be a 'VICTORY' not only to humanity, but also, to the animals (non-humans) by opening a door in Society's Mind to realize and practice <u>EMPATHY</u> by understanding the concept of PAIN for ALL living, breathing, and FEELING beings.

Sentience is the ability to feel, perceive, or to experience subjectively. To be sentient is to be conscious or self-aware, capable of perception or feeling. (14) Sentience is the quality or state of elementary consciousness such as sensations and emotions. (11) Princeton University Professor Peter Singer calls beings with the capacity to experience pleasures and

PAINS sentient. The fact that sentience is the capacity of being able to experience feelings is reinforced by the statement made by Professor John Webster, University of Bristol, when he stated, " A sentient animal (non-human) is one for which feelings matter." (14) Sentience in all animals (non-humans) is as obvious as rain is wet and the sun is warm. (71)

"It is so very clear to understand all the unending PAIN and suffering that animals (non-humans) consistently endure just so the selfish, uncaring, calloused society of humans can satisfy their unnecessary vile desires." Opal Dockery

Eighteenth-century philosophers used the concept of sentience to distinguish the ability to think (reason) from the ability to feel (sentience). In modern Western philosophy, sentience is the ability to experience sensations. (14) Sentient beings feel sensations such as **PAIN** and pleasure. (37) When a being is sentient, he will naturally have interests. For instance, the capacity for sentient beings to feel **PAIN** provides him with an interest in not feeling **PAIN**. (7) Such is observed regarding cows who will walk around an electric fence because they have an interest in avoiding the **PAIN** of the fence. (6) A direct duty to an animal (non-human) is one we have because the animal (non-human) itself has some interest, for example, to be nourished and avoid torture and **PAIN**. (14)

"I have never yet happened upon a trace of evidence...to show that any one animal was

made for another as much as it was made for itself." John Muir (18)

It is necessary to acknowledge the fact that all animals (non-humans) experience **PAIN**. (6) An enormous amount of scientific research reveals a direct relevance to the treatment of human **PAIN** that is conducted on animals (non-humans), discovering they respond well to **PAIN**. (8)

Animals (non-humans) have nervous systems very similar to humans, which respond physiologically like ours. Therefore, when the animal (non-human) is in circumstances in which we would feel **PAIN**, an initial rise of blood pressure, dilated pupils, perspiration, and increased pulse rate exits. Also, if the stimulus continues, a fall in blood pressure will be quite evident. (31)

"Society is capable of functioning quite well without inflicting PAIN on the animal kingdom. But our so-called civilization is too uncaring and desensitized at this point in time for this to be accomplished."
Opal Dockery

People often behave in certain ways which is a direct result of their emotional state such as crying, fighting, or fleeing. Some think that since animals (non-humans) do not react comparable to humans as a result of an emotion shows they do not have the capability to experience or possess emotions. (48) Due to the fact that we cannot ask animals (non-humans) questions, it is necessary to make observations and come to reasonable conclusions. (38) So many judgments regarding the similarity between human and animal (non-human) behavior are readily made by ordinary observers. (31) William James, in his article 'What Is An Emotion?' (Mind, 9, 1884:188-205), argued that emotional experiences are due to the experience of bodily changes. The perception of bodily changes as they occur is emotion. (48) The reactions of many animals (non-humans) to bodily events that humans would report as

PAINFUL are easily and automatically recognized as **PAIN** responses such as high pitched vocalizations, fear responses, nursing of injuries, and learned avoidance which are among the responses of many animals (non-humans). (31)

"The question is not, Can they reason? nor Can they talk? but, Can they suffer?" Jeremy Bentham (1789) – An introduction to the Principles of Morals and Legislation. (9)

PAIN is a state of consciousness, a 'mental event'. Behavioral signs of **PAIN** include writhing, facial contortions, moaning, yelping, or other forms of calling, attempts to avoid the source of the **PAIN**, and appearance of fear at the prospect of its repetition. (31) Physical and emotional **PAIN** have been studied in terms of an animal's (non-human's) body language, vocalization, temperament, depression, locomotion, immobility, and clinical changes in cardiovascular, respiratory, nervous, and muscular systems. Awareness of these emotions allows veterinarians to administer appropriate **PAIN** relief to their patients. (5)

"A very good definition of suffering in a sentient being is from Buddhists who state that

everything/everyone wants to live and nothing/no one wants to feel PAIN. Anything that causes PAIN or death causes suffering." (18)

Even though society is fully aware that all animals (non-humans) experience emotions and **PAIN**, they make a conscious decision to blatantly use them for their own personal pleasures and convenience due to the fact that they mistakenly believe this is necessary for human survival. Animals (non-humans) most certainly do have feelings. Those who deny this fact do so in order to justify their own treatment of animals (non-humans). Animal (non-human) rights implies that animals (non-humans) should undoubtedly be used for no other purpose than for the benefit of the animals (non-humans) themselves. (12)

"Man serves the interest of no creature but himself."
George Orwell (44)

Dr. Marion Dawkins, ethologist and professor of animal (non-human) behavior at the University Of Oxford, stresses the importance of thinking regarding animal (non-human) welfare not simply in terms of what humans would like for animals (non-humans), but in terms of what the animals (non-humans) would like for themselves. She further states,

"The point is this, if emotions reside in our bodies, then they must reside in animals' (non-humans') bodies, too; since humans and animals (non-humans) share the same biology." To paraphrase Charles Darwin, the difference is one of degree, not one of a kind. (13)

"The love of all living creatures is the most noble attribute of man." Charles Darwin (43)

All animals (non-humans) undoubtedly do deserve moral consideration; since they are sentient such as possessing the capacity to feel **PAIN**. The morally safe position is to give them the benefit of the doubt, if there is uncertainty about animals

(non-humans) being sentient. (8)
     During the question and answer period at a symposium which was held at the Smithsonian Institution in October, 2000, a former program leader from the National Science Foundation asked Cynthia Moss, "How do you know these animals (non-humans) are feeling the emotions you claim that are?" and Cynthia aptly replied, "How do you know they're not?" It's about time that the skeptics and naysayers had to prove their claims that animals (non-humans) do not experience emotions. (5) Ones who deny the emotions of animals (non-humans) have never sought to observe and accept this fact which is evidenced by scientific as well as 'common sense observation'. (29)

"The 'Burden Of Proof' should be on those who deny it." (75)

There are huge obstacles in applying the knowledge we now know about animal (non-human) sentience to the real world. The reason for this has to do with coming to terms with the inhumanity of the Western world. The European Union is on the right track regarding animal (non-human) sentience. In 1997, the concept of animal (non-human) sentience was written into the basic law of the European Union. The legally binding protocol annexed to the Treaty of Amsterdam recognizes that animals (non-humans) are "sentient beings", and requires the EU and its member states to "pay full regard to the welfare requirements of animals (non-humans)". (14)

"Anything that can suffer is sentient and anything sentient is deserving of rights." (41)

The concept of sentience is central to the philosophy of animals' (non-humans') rights because sentence is necessary for the ability to suffer which is held to entail certain rights. (27) The basis of animal (non-human) rights is the recognition that animals (non-humans) are sentient beings. This means they are capable of being aware of sensations and emotions, feeling **PAIN** and suffering, as well as experiencing a state of well being. Our own behavior towards

animals (non-humans) should be
guided by the recognition of the
fact that they are sentient
beings. (8)

**"We need to finally
accept that all sentient
creatures are deserving
of basic rights, I define
basic rights as this – the
ability to pursue life
without having someone
else's will involuntarily
forced upon you."
Moby (18)**

Nothing has ever attributed as
low a status as animals
(non-humans) are given by
humans. Their given status
lowers their basic rights to live
and their rights to be free from
attributions that we make for our

own ends. (8) Those who advocate animal (non-human) rights are told that they are too emotional. Yet, since emotions are the hallmark of our humanity, perhaps they are vital to sorting out the actions that are needed to bring peace to this planet for ourselves and the rest of all creation, human or non-human. (15) It is imperative to acknowledge the fact that the correct approach to animal (non-human) rights holds that the only characteristic necessary for basic rights consideration is sentience which is a moral matter. (14)

"Shame on such a morality that is worthy of pariahs, and fails to recognize that eternal existence that exists in every living being, and

shines forth with
inscrutable significance
from all eyes that see
the sun."
Arthur Schopenhauer
(1788-1860) (18)

David Pearce is a British
philosopher of the negative
utilitarian school of ethics. He is
most famous for his advocation of
the idea that there exits a strong
ethical imperative for humans to
work towards the abolition of
suffering in all sentient beings.
(14) Animals (non-humans)
cannot defend themselves; so
society uses them for their own
benefit. (69) Our treatment of
animals (non-humans) is a form
of slavery which is proven by the
confinement, breeding, and
killing of them. (70)

"As a custodian of the planet it is our responsibility to deal with all species with kindness, love, and compassion. That these animals suffer through human cruelty is beyond understanding. Please help to stop the madness."
Richard Gere (18)

Professor Gary L. Francione's approach to animal (non-human) rights, in his book *Introduction to Animal Rights: Your Child or the Dog,* holds that the only characteristic that is necessary for basic rights consideration is sentience (14) as well as another basic right to not be the property of others, human or nonhuman. (37) Isn't just the fact that they are alive sufficient for us to leave animals (non-humans) alone? They should have the right to live out their lives just as we do. (5)

"Life Force is present all around us. Is a human being's life force more valuable than an animal's? How can one look at an animal and not realize that it has emotions comparable to a human?"
Opal Dockery

It is a higher level of philosophy which advocates that one must rise above the mistakes of the past in an effort to reach a higher level of Thought and Being. The really important moral issues in animal's (non-human's) welfare arise precisely due to the belief held by much of society that animals (non-humans) do have conscious emotional experiences. (16)

The topic of consciousness regarding animals (non-humans) remains a matter of common sense to most people that animals (non-humans) do have conscious experiences. Conscientiousness in animals (non-humans) is exhibited in their ability to perceive and respond to many features of their environments. Most people, if asked why they think familiar animals (non-humans) such as their pets are conscious, would point to similarities between the behavior of those animals (non-humans) and human behavior.

"Animals share with us the privilege of having a Soul." Pythagoras (18)

Many philosophers maintain that consciousness is not explainable in familiar scientific terms. Although it has been suggested many times that conscientiousness cannot be explained in scientific terms, naturalistic observation of animal (non-human) behavior has proven they possess conscientiousness. Such behavioral criteria should be the basis of proof that animals (non-humans) possess conscientiousness. Despite all solid attempts to prove that animals (non-humans) possess consciousness, this topic remains controversial and even taboo among scientists, even while it remains a matter of common sense that animals (non-humans) do have many conscious experiences. (8)

"The fact that man knows right from wrong proves his intellectual superiority to the other creatures, but the fact that he can do wrong proves his moral inferiority to any creatures that cannot." *What Is Man?, 1906* **Mark Twain (18)**

Consciousness is applied when one is awake rather than asleep as well as the basic ability of perceiving and responding to selected features of one's environments enabling one with the ability to be aware of those features. (8) A vast amount of animals (non-humans) possess consciousness as in planning, categorization, and reasoning. Oliver Wendell Holmes observed that dogs can tell the difference between intentional aggression and a benign mistake. He wrote, "Even a dog distinguishes between being stumbled over and being kicked." (6)

What animals (non-humans) feel is more important than what they know when we consider what sorts of treatment are permissible. It does not take much intellectual effort to experience **PAIN**, feeling, or hunger. (16)

"Reverence for life applies to all living beings."
Albert Schweitzer (35)

It is the human belief that we have the absolute right to command all other species, simply because we have the possession of opposite physical characteristics as well as various levels of mental abilities. Humanity feels that such attitudes authorize us to decide how animals (non-humans) should live and die while blatantly disregarding the fear and **PAIN** they experience. Such attitudes grants us the ability to set limits on their level of comfort and natural behavior. And because we insist that our intelligence holds more importance than that of other species, we have removed ourselves from any accountability. That alone not only displays humanity's lack of **EMPATHY**, but is inherently dangerous. (6)

"To my mind, the life of a lamb is no less precious than that of a human being. I should be unwilling to take the life of a lamb for the sake of the human body."
Mahatma Gandhi (18)

Although the degree of cognitive abilities should not be a consideration of the value of being sentient such as a being's ability to experience pleasure and **PAIN**, the search for animal (non-human) consciousness is frequently seen as the search for higher and higher cognitive abilities in animals (non-humans) which Professor Peter Singer states that this so-called "hierarchy of intelligence" must cease. If the principle of equality among humans were based on their attributes, as some believe we should do with animals (non-humans), we would see that people are plainly not identical in their abilities and attributes. If intelligence is a barometer to determine equality, then humans with a higher IQ should rule over those with a lower one. (6) So while some say, "If we cannot measure it, it does not exist." Someday we may be able to understand more of the things we cannot measure. But until then, we need to accept them. (25) One can be conscious of a headache or the fear of flying without being able to put the experience into words or reason about it. (16)

"The greatness of a nation and its moral progress can be measured

by the way its animals are treated."
Mahatma Gandhi (63)

Language is not a measure or requirement of intelligence or conscientiousness. Animals (non-humans) can communicate with humans even though they cannot speak our language, very similar to mentally challenged people who cannot speak but can communicate. (8)

Professor Peter Singer states that just because animals (non-humans) do not possess such qualities as extreme intelligence and highly complex language, does not mean that they are not sentient beings due the fact that these qualities are not present in the young or mentally disabled humans. The only distinction is a prejudice based on species alone, which is called speciesism because it differentiates humans from other animals (non-humans) purely on the grounds that they are human. An exceptionally clever individual does not have the right to exploit the less clever individuals of his own species. So in the same context, just because one species is more clever than the other, does not give it the right to imprison and torture the other. (15)

"I am the 'voice for the voiceless'; Through me the dumb shall speak, Till the deaf world's ears be made to hear, The wrongs of the wordless weak. And I am my brother's keeper, And I will fight his fights; And speak the

**words for beast and bird,
Till the world shall set
things right." Ella
Wheeler Wilcox (26)**

Although animals (non-humans) cannot express their feelings linguistically, researchers have found that like humans, their emotions can be expressed through actions. It is so obvious that every animal (non-human) has its own form of body language. (23) The ability to understand another animal's (non-human's) communication, and how to respond to it, is a very strong indicator of animal (non-human) sentience. (19)

An example of animal (non-human) communication was displayed by a mother duck in Vancouver, British Columbia.

When a family of ducklings fell down a Vancouver sewer grate, their mother did what any parent would do. She got help from a passing police officer.

Vancouver police officer Jay Peterson admitted he was not sure what to make of the duck that grabbed him by the pant leg while he was on foot patrol on Wednesday evening in a neighborhood near the city's downtown.

"I thought it was a bit goofy, so I shoved it away," Peterson told the Vancouver Sun newspaper.

The mother duck persisted, grabbing Peterson's leg again when he tried to leave, and then wadding to a nearby sewer grate where she sat down and waited for him to follow and investigate.

"I went up to where the duck was lying and saw eight little babies in the water below," he said.

Police said they removed the heavy metal grate with the help of a tow truck and used a vegetable strainer to lift the ducklings to safety.

Mother and offspring then departed for a nearby pond. (30)

Even though language is not a measure of intelligence or consciousness, it may be necessary for abstract thought but has nothing to do with experiencing **PAIN**. (31) There is a school of thought that the conscious experience of emotions is far older in evolutionary time than the ability to form concepts and certainly than to use language. (13)

Our treatment of the great apes raises questions about the principles which underlay human equality. The cognitive capacities of great apes can rival or surpass those of very young children and humans with severe cognitive deficits. Should the interests of the great apes who can use sign language be considered over infants and mentally challenged people who cannot even communicate? (6)

Human infants and young children are unable to use language, but we do not deny that they can suffer. (31) It has been proven that orangutans can learn how to use language at the level of a three year old child.

In 1978, an adult female orangutan named Rinnie experienced the feeling of affection (lust) toward her human keeper. He taught her sign language and could not believe how fast she learned it; but she took the tutoring personally. One day Rinnie took him by the hand and tried to seduce him. He pushed her away. After this, she lost all interest in signing.

This incident suggests that orangutans can learn to communicate through sign language as well as develop interpersonal connections with humans and engage in long-term planning which is evidenced from the fact that following her keeper's unwillingness to accept her sexual offer, she displayed an ongoing grudge which led to her refusing to no longer communicate.

In the early 1970's, a gorillla named Koko learned the elements of sign language at Stanford University. Koko had advanced further with language than any animal (non-human), possessing a working vocabulary of over one thousand signs as well as understanding, approximately, two thousand words of spoken English. Koko laughed at her own jokes and those of others, cried when hurt or left alone, and talked about her feelings, using words like happy, sad, afraid, enjoy, eager, frustrate, mad, and quite frequently, love. She also participated in an online chat session.

Two incidents have proven that Koko possessed the emotion of mourning. She became close and would cuddle a cat that she named All-Ball. Koko grieved when told that All-Ball was hit by a car and killed. When Michael, a gorilla who had been Koko's companion for twenty four years died of natural causes, she uttered frequent, mournful cries, especially at night in the weeks after his death. She did not want to be left alone and indicated with

sign language that she wanted a
light left on at night when she
went to bed. (6)

It has been proven several
times that animals (non-humans)
possess characteristics that are
comparable emotionally
to humans as well as having
personalities quite similar to us.
Samuel Gosling, who is a biologist
at the University of Texas at
Austin, said that there are, at least,
four dimensions of several
animal's (non-human's)
personality. These include
sociability, affection, emotional
stability, and competence. He
also states that these dimensions
are 'remarkably' similar to the four
basic categories of human
personality found in standard
psychological tests. (4)

"If a group of beings from another planet were to land on Earth – beings who considered themselves as superior to you as you feel yourself to be to other animals – would you concede them the rights over you that you assume over other animals?"
George Bernard Shaw
(18)

Though animals surely do feel **PAIN**, our confidence in our ability to understand and evaluate the experiences of another being drops off as the being becomes more unlike ourselves. (6) There is no reason to believe that natural selection shapes only physical traits. Naturalist Charles Darwin argued that emotions exist in animals (non-humans), and his evolutionary theory suggests that behavioral traits, including personality, can evolve in just the same way as fins, wings, and arms. (11)

"The Soul is the same in all living creatures, although the body of each is different." Hippocrates (18)

A 2007 study in Canada found that animals (non-humans) have their own separate personalities. We should realize that studying the personality of animals (non-humans) could help us understand a lot about human personality. Many instances of personality exist in several animals (non-humans) that is quite similar to human personality. (17)

Nature does not carve a sharp dividing line between humans and the rest of the animal (non-human) kingdom. (6) Humans are very genetically related to mice and rats. That is why mice are such a powerful model for human disease research and testing for drugs. (34)

The DNA of humans and chimpanzees are more than 98% identical. As a matter of fact, chimpanzees have a closer relationship to humans than they do gorillas. (6) It has been discovered that personality characteristics such as the conscientiousness vs. impulsiveness factor of personality (deliberation, self-discipline, dutifulness, order) might be evident only in humans and their closest relatives, chimpanzees. (8)

Washoe (1965-2007), was a chimpanzee who was the first non-human to learn to use a human language, that of American Sign Language. She could reliably use about two hundred fifty signs. It is believed that with human children, affection and feelings of love are important in cognitive developmental. (6) Such was projected to Washoe to the extent that her first sentence was, "Let me out of here." (36)

Washoe also exhibited evidence of retaining long-term memory. At the age of five years old, she was transferred from the care of Allen and Beatrice Gardner, who had taught her American Sign Language, in order to be transferred to a primate institute. There was an eleven year period that she was separated from the Gardners after which they made a surprise visit to Washoe. Washoe remembered and spontaneously signed their names. She signed 'COME MRS G' to Beatrice Gardner, then led her into an adjoining room and began to play a game with her which she had not played since she was five years old. (6)

Loulis, a chimpanzee, is the first non-human to ever learn a human language from another non-human. He was able to acquire ASL from Washoe. The details of this research can be found in "Teaching Sign Language To Chimpanzees" edited by Allen and Beatrice Gardner. (73)

Due to the fact that chimpanzees can have such

long-term memories suggests the possibility they also possess a fairly broad conception of life. This gives us reason to acknowledge the fact that they do not live merely from day-to-day but reflect on events of the past and probably of the future. (6)

It has long been known that chimpanzees can use mirrors to inspect their images. Gallup proved mirror self-recognition is an indicator of self-awareness. He anesthetized chimpanzees and marked their foreheads with a distinctive dye. Upon waking, marked animals (non-humans) who were allowed to see themselves in a mirror touched their own foreheads in the region of the mark significantly more than ones who were not marked. This task gives reason to maintain that chimpanzees possess consciousness, which further supports the fact that we should develop **EMPATHY** toward animals (non-humans) regarding their feelings. When considering the fact that humans are primates, it is logical to conclude that animals (non-humans) have emotions very comparable to humans. (8)

The link between humans and animals (non-humans) may be closer than previously thought, according to research by Dr. Filippo Aurell, leader in Animal Behavior and Co-Director of LJMU's Research Center In Evolutionary Anthropology And Palaeoecology. He presented his research in 2005 at the BA Festival Of Science In Dublin. His research found that our furry relatives may share many of the same emotions that humans experience in everyday life. (65)

Animals (non-humans) are so closely related to humans emotionally that drugs are utilized in experiments in order to model behavior and emotions including anger, stress, and fear. As with humans, fear in animals (non-humans) raises heart-rate and blood pressure. (64)

The brain of a human and that of an animal (non-human) is extremely comparable regarding the most ancient of all emotions, fear. (39) Defranco reinforces this fact by stating that animals (non-humans) definitely have primary emotions like fear. Both humans and animals (non-humans) have, in the center of their brains, an almond-shaped structure named the amygdala, which is closely linked to fear as well as other emotions. When this area is damaged, normal responses to danger are not experienced, resulting in one becoming unable to experience fear when placed in dangerous situations. (32)

A vast amount of scientists have argued that animals (non-humans) are not fully capable of suffering due to the fact that they cannot anticipate future events. But many animals (non-humans) often display fear or aggression when approached by an experimenter. This proves that emotions cannot exist in a vacuum, but are part of a response to external factors.

Many laboratory animals (non-humans) show aberrant behavior such as self-mutilation and feces-eating due to their sterile environment. These are signs of stress and depression. It is recognized that animals (non-humans) suffer in these conditions as well as others such as zoos, when animals (non-humans) exhibit behavioral emotions like repetitive pacing, rocking, and psychological problems. (39)

Animals (non-humans) certainly aren't unfeeling objects. They don't like being shocked, cut up, starved, chained, stunned, crammed into tiny cages, tied up, ripped away from family and friends, or isolated. (5)

"If you don't want to be beaten, imprisoned, mutilated, killed or tortured then you shouldn't condone such behavior towards anyone, be they human or not." Moby (18)

Goddall says that scientists who use animals (non-humans) to study the human brain, then deny that they have feelings, are "illogical". (28) Jean Swingle Greek, a veterinary consultant, gave an opinion regarding animals (non-humans) who are used for experimental purposes by stating, "Either the emotions of animals (non-humans) are like man's, in which case it is wrong to subject them to such tests, or the animals' (non-humans') emotional lives are so different from man that studying their response in the lab is unlikely to ever yield any tangible gains for human health. They simply cannot have it both ways." (4) If there is uncertainty about whether other animals (non-humans) really are conscious, the morally safe position is to give them the benefit of the doubt. (8)

"If man is not to stifle human feelings, he must practice kindness toward animals, for he who is cruel to animals becomes hard also in his dealings with man. We can judge the heart of a man by his treatment of animals."
Immanual Kant (76)

Scientists once scoffed, but now they are coming around. Various scientists are not saying that animals (non-humans) do not have feelings as well as the ability to think. What they are saying is that this is not a subject they care to think about and is quite difficult to scientifically prove. Also, they do not want to create a discontent with their fellow scientists; so they remain silent. But a growing number of scientists do agree that animals (non-humans) are conscious and capable of experiencing basics emotions. Even though it is hard scientifically, to prove that animals (non-humans) have feelings, which is true, one must consider the fact that it is also difficult to prove scientifically that humans have feelings. (42)

"I wish that medical researchers who experiment on animals would experiment on humans to try to find a cure for their insensitivity to the suffering of animals". Rhonda Stagg (79)

Science is but one way of knowing and not the only show in town. It is nonsense to claim that we do not know if animals (non-humans) feel **PAIN** or have a point of view about whether they like or do not like being exposed to certain treatments. The eyes tell it all, and if we can stand it, we should look into the fear-filled eyes of animals (non-humans) who suffer at our hands. Dare to look into the sunken eyes of animals (non-humans) who are afraid or feeling other sorts of **PAIN**, and then try to deny to yourself and others that these individuals aren't feeling ANYTHING! (5)

"Who Can Believe There Is No Soul Behind The Eyes?"
Theophile Gautier (61)

Researchers have discovered that most emotions are accompanied by the production of certain brain chemicals not only in humans, but also, in animals (non-humans). When animals (non-humans) are scared, the brain produces chemicals that make them alert and ready to flee, while happy thoughts cause the brain to release chemicals that soothe and calm. For instance, your dog's tail wags when you go out to the porch and play with him. That is his way of expressing happiness and joy. It is similar to when cats purr. (45)

"I think of 'The Mystery Of Animals'. Man seeks to destroy that which he does not understand sometimes. So WHO

understands the mind of an animal? That animal does!" Opal Dockery

So many people do not understand animals' (non-humans') emotions. (22) Animals (non-humans), like us, come into the world pre-equiped with a number of emotions that help them adapt and survive. (38) By and large, emotions are the ONE basic thing we have in common with animals (non-humans). Reasoning ability is what sets us apart. Obviously, not all animals (non-humans), let alone species of animals (non-humans), have the same emotions; but emotions can be located in the brain, and other animals (non-humans) seem to be wired up very much the same way as ourselves as far as emotions are concerned. (45)

In humans there are six emotions, fear, disgust, desire (lust), sadness, happiness, anger and rage, linked to particular brain areas as well as hormonal and chemical responses. These are survival responses that protect us from adverse conditions and cause us to seek out favorable conditions. Most are linked to our perception of comfort and discomfort. (33) Animals (non-humans) definitely possess equivalent physiological responses to the same or similar stimuli. Also, there is growing evidence that they have secondary emotions like love, jealousy, and greed. (38)

Pet owners have long believed their animal (non-human) companions loved them back. Everyone who ever owned a pet has at least one story, usually many, telling how it seems just as emotional as any human. How many times have we heard a pet owners say, "He is scared of that?" or "He hates being left behind?" They have deciphered their pet's emotions and supporting the possibility of such animal (non-human) having the same sort of emotion as their own. (75)

Bowlingual is a computer based dog-to-human language translator device that categorizes a dog's bark into one of six distinct emotions (happy, sad, frustrated, on-guard, assertive, and needy) which displays the corresponding emotion on the screen. This proves that dogs possess emotions. Otherwise the device would not work. (46)

Another device which proves emotions in dogs is a mobile carrier. The dog barks into a phone which is translated into a text, also, revealing six emotions: happy, sad, cheerful, needy, threatened, and assertive. (47)

Several emotions have been observed in animals (non-humans). Sheep can remember faces for up to two years. When isolated from their flock, they experience stress, but being shown pictures of familiar sheep faces reduces their feelings of anxiety. Another example of memory possessed by animals (non-humans) are cows who can recognize familiar faces. (13) The capacity of memory has been observed in cats that no longer flee from the sound of a vacuum cleaner, but simply move to a vantage point such as a book case. (39)

A 'sense of self' and memory is proven by cows who have escaped slaughterhouses where they were sold, finding their way back home after days of walking and avoiding challenges such as electric fences. (20)

Grief is a common emotion among animals (non-humans) and is quite prominent in the wild, particularly, following the death of a mate, parent, offspring, or close companion. In Tanzania, behavior of a fifty year old chimpanzee was observed. Throughout the following day, her son sat beside her lifeless body, occasionally, taking her hand and whimpering. Over the next few weeks, he grew increasingly listless and withdrawn as well as refusing food, despite his siblings' efforts to bring him back. Three weeks after his mother's death, the formerly healthy young chimp dies from grief. (28)

Several animals (non-humans) express sadness by mourning for their dead including gorillas, llamas, and elephants. The gorilla, Koko, displayed separation anxiety in the form of sadness, depression, and mourning when her friends, the cat All-Ball and the gorilla Michael passed away. It was reported that after a twenty seven year old llama died of old age, his lifelong partner died next to him for no apparent cause. The effect on the remaining two llama's was grave. One stood across the fence stoic for the next two days staring at the hole in the ground. Another stayed in his little barn and wailed for two days. On the third day, they both emerged from their wailing and resumed their normal activities. Not only do elephants mourn, they also make graves by breaking branches to cover their dead which displays the capability of reasoning. (6)

It has been proven numerous times regarding the intelligence of pigs. Amy Hatkoof relates the intelligence of pigs who can fetch objects upon request. She also tells of a pig who was taught video games with a joy stick. This experiment is described in the June 1998 edition of ANIMAL PEOPLE. (62)

EMPATHY and reasoning ability regarding mice was

reported from CeAnn Lambert who runs the Indiana Coyote Rescue Center in Bringhurst. One morning she noticed two baby mice trying to get out of a deep sink in her garage. Seeing their growing frustration, she put a lid of water in the sink. The livelier one went over to get a drink and on his way found a piece of food which it picked up and took back to the weaker mouse. Every time the weaker pup tried to take a bite, the other moved the food gradually towards the water until finally the exhausted animal (non-human) reached it. Their strength renewed, both were then able to climb out using a board Lambert had placed in the sink.

Bears have similar emotional depths. In September, 2005 in

Homer, Alaska an article reported two bear cubs who stuck together after their mother had been shot. The male cub had been wounded, causing him to limp and swam very slowly, but his sister was seen hauling salmon out of the river for him to eat. The young female obviously cared for her brother, and her support was crucial for his survival. This is a pure example of his sister exhibiting reasoning ability as well as **EMPATHY**.

Another example of **EMPATHY** was seen in a group of elephants at Samburg National Reserve in Northern Kenya, who were adjusting their behavior regarding an elephant who walked very slowly due to being crippled. The other elephants would walk awhile and look around to see where she was. Depending on how she was doing, they would either wait or continue. They never left her behind. Out of friendship and **EMPATHY** they adjusted their behavior for her to remain in the group. Their kindness and care were unconditional. (49)

Disgust can be observed in some animals (non-humans) in relation to their avoidance of various undesirable things such as stale food. (80) Desire (Lust) is associated with the basic mating urge such as arousal which is present in both humans and animals (non-humans). (39) Love arises from a profound oneness such as bonding in a familial manner which exists in many animals (non-humans) with other animals (non-humans) as well as

humans. (52) Many animals
(non-humans) exhibit the emotion
of love, as observed in the great
apes, who have adopted infants
unrelated to them. (77) The
actions of the orangutan Rennie,
is an excellent example of lust
and, possibly, love when she
refused to sign after her keeper
refused her sexual advances. (6)

Affection and submission can
be comparable to happiness which
is observed in domesticated
animals (non-humans) when they
allow the owner to pet, groom, and
play with them. This is also
evident when cats roll on their
backs as a result of their owners
returning home. (39)

Playing proves to exhibit a
numerous amount of emotions in
animals (non-humans). Joy is

apparent when animals (non-humans) are playing with one another or with people. Also, joy is one of the most obvious emotions which is also considered pleasure and happiness. Anyone who has ever held a purring cat or been greeted by a barking, tail-waging dog knows that animals (non-humans) often appear to be happy. (28)

Happiness is observed as contentment which is evident when they play. There is evidence that playing releases "feel-good" hormones in the brain, giving a sense of well-being. This self-fulfilling behavior can be observed when an animal (non-human) smiles with his eyes or wags its tail. (45)

Another example of the

"feel-good" chemical is the emotion of pleasure which is one of the most obvious in most animals (non-humans). A good example is exhibited when your cat snuggles up purring. (39)

Euphoria has been observed in animals (non-humans) as a result of being administered drugs. Drugs that alternate brain chemistry is the same in animals (non-humans) as humans which further validates the fact that they possess emotions comparable us. (52)

Anger is evidenced in many animals (non-humans) such as a dog who growls and shows his teeth and a cat whose fur stands on end. (39) Animals (non-humans) who are handled against their will display the fight reaction as a result of anger. Such animals (non-humans) often remain angry even when the stimulus is removed, displaying the capability of memory. (57)

Bulls express aggression by bunting or striking a challenger with his head. An aggressive bull will turn his body perpendicular to a challenger to display his full height and length. Many farmers resort to artificial insemination as a result of aggressiveness displayed by bulls. (59)

Rage is an emotion which is closely connected to the anticipatory rewards of feeling. It has been observed that when certain animals (non-humans) are stimulated regarding rewards, a feeling of pleasure is evident. When such stimulus is withdrawn, the animal (non-human) may bite. This is a response to an unfulfilled expectation and is known as the "frustration-aggression hypothesis" which might explain why an animal (non-human) might lash out when being pleasurably groomed. This is usually explained as the anxiety response, but it is possible that pleasurable sensations overflow into the rage emotion causing the animal (non-human) to automatically lash out.

Frustration is a result of being unable to perform natural behavior patterns. It is sometimes expressed in humans by crying. Animals (non-humans) express frustration in various forms such as shrieking, stamping, or tearing vegetation. Cats exhibit frustration when looking behind a window at a bird outside by the chattering of teeth which is a frustrated form of the neck. (39)

Curiosity regarding cows was observed by comedian Dave Allen in one of his BBC TV programs when he laid on his back in a field of cows. They all gathered around him. He also tried something similar by standing in the same place without moving for several minutes in a field of cows. They gathered around him again. In both incidents, the cows displayed their curiosity of never seeing anyone lying on their back in the field as well as standing in the same spot and not moving for several minutes. (57)

Urination is a common form of communication utilized by several animals (non-humans) in order to express their feelings regarding such emotions as spite and jealous. Spite was displayed from an overconfident, bullying male baboon who urinated on a female baboon's head because she resisted his advances.(49) Jealously has been observed in many animals (non-humans) such as a cat urinating on the bed as a result of a new family member. He wants to mix his scent with the owners and as well as claim his territory. (39)

Depression is a form of continued unhappiness which can be the result of **PAIN**. Chemical effects in the brain can cause the animal (non-human) to withdraw and, possibly, lose the will to live. The emotion of depression also has been observed regarding baby monkeys who crouched in a corner due to a very long-term isolation. (24)

Calves experience depression when they are affected by the emotional **PAIN** of separation from their mother. Abrupt and early weaning is distressing for the calf. Such calves will engage in repetitive crying and sometimes display a decline in their willingness to eat solid food. (6) Depression is also evident in mother cows whose calves have been taken away. They will walk up and down in an agitated way calling out and, apparently, looking for their calves. (57)

Oxytocin, a hormone associated with human social bonding, is important in giving mother animals (non-humans) the inclination to care for their babies.

(66) This is evidenced by observation regarding mother cats whose kittens have been taken away and destroyed, displaying a great deal of depression, frustration, and grief. They look for their kittens for many days with continued pacing and crying out.

Such has been seen regarding the contact between a mother cow and her newborn calf for a period as brief as five minutes which resulted in a strong specific maternal bond. (39) The effects of Oxycotin is also evidenced in an overprotective mother cow who will knock anyone down who gets in the way of her and her baby calf. (57)

The mother duck in Vancouver who obtained help from the police officer to rescue her babies is a pure example of maternal bonding as with human mothers relating to Oxycotin. (30)

The neural mechanisms for attachment and sadness regarding animals (non-humans) are beginning to be understood. When they are no longer able to spend time together because of death or separation, the loving animal (non-human) will visibly suffer and act in ways that convey sadness. (78)

Sadness has been observed regarding cows crying in slaughterhouses. Such was seen in the pregnant cow who cried and kneeled at the slaughterhouse, begging for her life. (54) This also

**displays the fact that
animals (non-humans)
are quite capable of
calculating the
future. (53)**

While researchers do not agree on how big a role social emotions play in the animal (non-human) world, there is widespread agreement that many animals (non-humans) share with humans the emotion of stress. (21) Stress is expressed in various ways with different animals (non-humans). Some are nervous and more easily stressed than others. Lisa Gould is a massage therapist for a wide variety of animals (non-humans) in Akron, Ohio. She administers massage for her patients to relieve stress. (58)

Observation of a cow's body language has been going on for centuries. Daniel Weary, an applied animal biologist at the University of British Columbus, demonstrated that dairy cows possess surprising intelligence and emotional sensitivity. He states that abrupt early weaning is distressing for both the calf and mother. Calves will engage in repetitive crying as well as a decline of eating solid food. (40)

The emotion of stress has been observed numerous times in cows by Charles Reader, who has been a farmer at Evenley near Brackley, Norhants for twenty eight years. He said, "All livestock are herd animals and they get a bit stressed if you separate them out." Researcher Krista McLennan pointed out that regrouping of cows is a problem, because there is a high level of stress among animals (non-humans) as they try to integrate into a new group. (74)

Animal (non-human) care has a profound effect on the emotion of temperament. An animal (non-human) with a nervous temperament is calm when in a familiar environment. He has learned that this environment is safe, but is more likely to panic when suddenly confronted with new things. However, if he discovers these new things himself, he is not as likely to be in the state of panic. (51)

Contentment has been observed in cows. It has been discovered that they produce more milk if they are contented. (59) Allowing pigs to rest one hour before slaughter as well as quiet handling will result in better meat because the quality of meat is negatively effected, which presents a result of poor flavor, if an animal (non-human) is stressed and experiences severe anxiety before slaughter. (60)

It is quite obvious that there cannot be an animal (non-humans) without sensations. (8) There is enough proof that animals (non-humans) lead an emotional life. Perhaps a much deeper one than most people are ready to accept. (75) The study of animal (non-human) emotions just may stir up some emotional storm in ourselves. (72)

It just might be that animals (non-humans) experience more vivid emotions than we do. (5) Why are we so special? Why are we such deeply feeling animals (humans) whereas other animals (non-humans) are not? Is it so difficult to accept that we should not be the standard against which other animals (non-humans) are compared? (8)

Lack of full scientific certainty should not be used as an excuse to delay taking action on this issue. We know enough to make informed decisions about animal (non-human) emotions and animal (non-human) sentience and why they matter.

The scientist, Marc Bekoff, states that he cannot even "prove" that humans experience emotions, but can only deduce how they are feeling through body language and facial expression. He can tell by observation the emotions animals (non-humans) are experiencing and states that animal (non-human) emotions may actually be more knowable than those of humans because they do not filter their feelings the way we do. (28) Doctor James Kirkwood, chief executive and scientific director of the Universities' Federation for Animal Welfare told BBC News Online states, "Animal (non-human) sentience has been a matter of debate down the centuries. We can't even prove absolutely that another human being is sentient though it would obviously be unreasonable to assume they are not." (68)

The rise of animal-emotion studies is fantastic and long overdue. (49) The examples provided in this document undoubtedly displays the fact that animals (non-humans) do possess emotions that may not be exactly like humans, but are very comparable and should be considered and respected. (56) It is up to us as a civilized society to not only accept this fact but to constantly practice **EMPATHY** regarding animals (non-humans) in our daily lives.

"I do not know how good I am or what my life amounts to as far as serving an example to others. But it is my great desire to be of service to humanity which, in my opinion, includes the animals."
Opal Dockery

CONCLUSION

'The Evolution Of The Mind' can only be accomplished through the utilization of **EMPATHY** regarding the feelings of animals (non-humans). It is a sad state of affairs to realize that humanity is so uncaring and desensitized toward the cruel utilization of animals (non-humans) which has prevented it from mentally evolving to the level of **EMPATHY** for them. One who has developed **EMPATHY** knows it is also essential regarding animals (non-humans).

We must get to the **'Core Of Life'** and work toward peace in the world by realizing that it is unnecessary for us to inflict

PAIN on animals (non-humans) due to the fact that they possess emotions quite similar to humans. If we cannot be kind to our fellow species on a personal level, this unkindness will radiate outward in other areas of our lives. It is extremely paramount in the society of the human race to consider these facts and practice **EMPATHY** toward all animals (non-humans). It is of the utmost urgency that this must undoubtedly occur.

In mankind's quest for survival at the expense of animals (non-humans), another survival is realized, the **'Survival Of The Mind'**. This cannot be accomplished by the continual acceptance regarding the killing of these innocence

beings. People want to be good;
so they make laws regarding the
killing of animals (non-humans).
"You can kill them, but do it
humanely." So what is so
humane about killing?

Have we as a society lost our
ability regarding **EMPATHY**
which we utilize only when
convenient? Yes, it is quite
apparent that society as a whole
has callously displaced the
ability for **EMPATHY** when
considering the welfare of
animals (non-humans).
EMPATHY is consistently
absent as society blatantly
disregards the feelings,
emotions, and lives of animals
(non-humans) who are legally
killed for the use of human
consumption in whatever
manner desired regardless of the

known **PAIN** that is forced
upon them.

Only the chosen few are
treated with dignity and respect
such as pets and endangered
species. The feelings of many
others like farm and factory
housed animals (non-humans)
are ignored. Peace will never be
available until humanity changes
its treatment of animals
(non-humans) by realizing and
accepting the responsibility for
their vile actions regarding the
total disregard of
EMPATHY.

It is vitally essential that
EMPATHY toward all
animals (non-humans) must be
incorporated into the society of
the human race due to the fact
that animals (non-humans)
experience emotions comparable

to humans. Since by **'common sense observation'**, it is undoubtedly evident that their natural actions are extremely comparable to humans such as Breathing, Eating, Drinking, Sleeping, Yawning, Defecation, Procreation, and **PAIN** as well as possessing the same five senses, it is logical to conclude that they undoubtedly do possess emotions comparable to humans.

Due to the fact that animals (non-humans) are, without question, comparable to humans physically, experiments are consistently conducted on them as a benefit to the human race. Therefore, it is logical to conclude that animals (non-humans) possess emotions comparable to humans. This fact alone proves that they endure unnecessary

PAIN at the uncaring hands of the human race.

As a result of such true knowledge, the needless suffering of such animals (non-humans) must be discontinued for such things as food, clothing, experiments, or any other reason. The exception of self-defense is the only acceptable reason for killing animals (non-humans). It is of paramount importance that society seriously consider these facts and take action to prove that we most certainly are a caring, civilized, **EMPATHETIC** and compassionate society.

The human race needs to be held to the highest standards of compassion and goodness regarding the plight of animals (non-humans). This can only be accomplished through the practice of **EMPATHY** toward animals

(non-humans) which definitely
must be incorporated into the
society of the human race.

It is imperative that we evolve
into a kinder and gentler society
by exercising **EMPATHY**
regarding our association with
animals (non-humans). This can
be accomplished by discontinuing
the acceptable practice of turning
a blind eye to the suffering and
misery of animals (non-humans)
and realizing they are living,
feeling beings with emotions
comparable to us. It is vitally
important that we accept the
responsibility for the
consequences of our actions and
arm ourselves with the moral
justice that every living being
deserves by exercising the
concept of **EMPATHY** to all
animals (non-humans). (25)

It is essential that we do better

than our ancestors. Future generations will look back on us with shock and horror when discovering our treatment of animals (non-humans) and wonder how we ignorantly and uncaringly ignored what is so very obvious regarding animal (non-human) emotions which are undoubtedly comparable to humans. They will be shocked and wonder how we could ever impose the horrific amount of harm, suffering, and **PAIN** on these helpless, innocent individuals who were living, feeling, and breathing beings that constantly suffered at our hands when we utilized them for whatever we desired such as eating, wearing, and experimentation. (5) But they mostly will be amazed to know that our society

DID NOT EVEN CARE!!!

It is "imperative" that civilization remembers and practices the words of Ella Wheeler Wilcox.

"I am the 'voice for the voiceless'; Through me the dumb shall speak, Till the deaf world's ears be made to hear, The wrongs of the wordless weak. And I am my brother's keeper, And I will fight his fights; And speak the words for beast and bird, Till the world shall set things right." Ella Wheeler Wilcox (26)

WE MUST ALL BECOME 'THE VOICE FOR THE VOICELESS'!!!!

REFERENCES

In order for ones who are not accustomed to using references, I designed the following very 'simply':

Quote By Friedrich Nietzsche: <u>"Man Is The Cruelest Of All Animals." says…</u> <u>https;//www.gooodreads.com : quotes</u>
(1)

<u>Daniel H. Pink – "Empathy Is About Standing In Someone…"</u> <u>https;//www.grainyquote.com : quotes</u>
(2)

<u>"Hunter Loses Desire For Thrill Of The Kill"</u>
E-4 The Kansas City Star
Saturday, February 16, 1991, (c) Universal Press Syndicate Written By Lemuel T. Ward of Crisfield,

Md.
(3)

BUZZLE.COM - Intelligent Life On The Web
"Scientists' Discover Emotions In Animals"
By Patricia Collier
http://www.buzzle.com/editorials/8-10-2003-44071.asp
(4)

"Animal Emotions And Animal Sentience And Why They Matter: Blending 'ScienceSense' With Common Sense Compassion And Heart."
ByMarcVekoff
University Of Colorado, US
(5)

Standford Law Review, October, 2001
"Standing Upright: The Moral And Legal Standing Of Humans And Other Apes"
Copyright (c)2001 Board Of

Trustees Of The Leland Standford
Junior University
By Adam Kobler
http://cyrano.cmsu.edu:2074/resul
t/text.w1?
RP=/Welcome/WestlawCampus/de
fault.wl&R...
(6)

"Sentience Is Sufficient For Basic
Rights Protection"
By Eric Prescott
http://www.opposingviews.com/ar
guments/sentience-is-sufficient-
for-basic-rights-protection
(7)

Stanford Encyclopedia Of
Philosophy "Animal
Consciousness"
First Published Sat. Dec.23, 1995;
Substantive Revision Wed.
Nov. 15, 2006
http://plato.stanford.edu/entries/
consciousnessanimal/
(8)

"Animal Rights Philosophy –
Speaking of Research"
https;//speakingofresearch.com :
ar...
(9)

Federal Statutes – Animal Legal &
Historical Center
https://www.animallaw > statutes
(10)

"Animals Have Emotions And
Personalities – Zoology" - Brief
Article"
USA Today (Society for the
Advancement of Education), Dec,
2001
http://findarticles.com/articles/mi_
m1277/is_2679_
130/ai_81110793
(11)

"Ethics – Animal Ethics – Animal
Rights BBC"
https://www.bb.co.uk > rights_1
(12)

A.W.I. Quarterly
(Animal Welfare Institute)
"Animal Sentience And The
Evolution Of Emotion"
Story By Tracy Baslie
http://www.awionline.org/pubs/qu
arterly/05-54-2/542p67.htm
(13)

"Sentience"
Wikipedia, The Free Encyclopedia
http://en.wikipedia.org/w/index.ph
p?title=Sentience&printable=yes
(14)

NATURE OF ANIMALS
"Why Do Animals Need Rights?"
By Diane C. Nicholson
http://www.natureofanimals.com/a
rticle1006.html
(15)

"Animal Minds And Emotions"
American Zoologis, Dec 2000
By Dawkins, Marian Stamp

http://findarticles.com/p/articles/mi_qa3746/is_200012/ai_n8923018
(16)

CURRENT RESEARCH AND FINDINGS
http://en.wikpedia.org/wiki/Emotion_in_animals
(17)

"Animal Rights Quotes"
http://www.animalliberationfront.com/Saints/Authors/Quotes/SortQuotesPhilosLiter.htm
(18)

"Everything You Need To Know About Animal Communication – Start Here"
https://learnhowtotalktoanimals.com
(19)

"Animal Intelligence What They Know And You Don't"

September 9, 2010
By Fiona Carmondy, Collegian
Columnist
https://www.the
collegianur.com/2010/09/09/
animal-intelligence-what-they-
know-and-you-
don%E2...
(20)

NATURE
"Inside The Animal Mind"
http://www.pbs.org/wnet/nature/a
nimalmind/
emotion.html
(21)

HELIUM
"Emotion In Animals"
Pets And Animals > Dog's
Emotions
"Understanding Your Dog's
Emotions"
http://helium.com/items/112264-
people-understand-animals-
emotions
(22)

"The Art Of Body Language"
Sacramento Zoo – Sacraamento,
CA.
https://www.saczoo.org > 2017/12
(23)

"Pit Of Despair"
Wikipedia
https://www.en.m.wikipedia.org >
wiki
(24)

"Wild Justice: The Moral Lives Of
Animals By Marc Bekoff And…"
https://press.uchicago.edu >
Chicago
(25)

"Voice For The Voiceless"
By Ella Wheeler Wilcox (1850-
1919)
https://www.all-creatures > are-
ella
(26)

"If You Can't Measure It, Does It Exist?" - Quora
https://www.quora.com > if-somthi...
(27)

ANIMAL EMOTIONS
By Laura Tangley
From US News And World Report
30 October 2000
http://www.saveourstrays.com/feelings.htm
(28)

"The Tension Between Common Sense And Scientific Perception of..."
https://www.sciencedirect.com > ph
(29)

PEOPLE FOR THE ANIMAL RIGHTS
For The Animals
Box 8707 Kansas City, Missouri 64114
816-767-1199

Autumn 2001
www.parkc.org
(30)

"Do Animials Feel Pain?"
By Peter Singer
Excerpted From Animal
Liberation, 2nd Edition,
New York: Avon Books, 1950, pp.
10-12, 14-15
Acrobat Version
http://www.animal-rights-
library.com/texts-m/singer03.htm
(31)

HOME AGAIN – Pet Recovery
Service
"The Science Of Animal
Emotions"
ABCNews.com, November 08,
2003
By Pierre Thomas and the
ABCNEWS Investigative Unit
http://www.homeagainid.com/new
s/article.cfm?storyid=11577
(32)

"Emotions In Animals"
Wikipedia
https://en.m.wikipedia.org > wiki
(33)

"Study Finds Close Genetic Link
Between Humans Rodents"
Report Underscores Role Of Mice
In Drug Research
By Steve Sternberg
USA TODAY
(34)

Albert Schweitzer's "Reverence
For Life Philosophy And It's..."
https://www.clarkson.edu > news
> B...
(35)

"Washoe (chimpanzee)"
Wikipedia
https://en. m.wikipedia.org>wiki
(36)

SENTIENCE
From Wikipedia, The Free

Encyclopedia
http://en.wikipedia.urg/wiki/Sentience
(37)

EMOTIONAL DOGS
http://www.riverdeep.net/current/2001/09/091001_
dogs.jhtml
(38)

"DO CATS HAVE EMOTIONS?"
http://www.messybeast.com/emoticat.html
(39)

THE EMOTIONAL LIVES OF COWS
Mary Bates Science 06.30.14 12:12 PM
https://www.wired.com/2014/06/the-emotional-lives-of-dairy-cows/
(40)

"From Human Rights To Sentient Rights The Next Generation

Of…"
https://www.openingglobalrights.
org
(41)

JEFFREY MASSON: "On Science
And Animal Emotions"
http://www.animal-lib.org.au/
more_interviews/jeffreymasson/
(42)

Quotes By Charles Darwin: "The
Love For All Animals Is The
Most…"
https://www.goodreads.com >
quotes
(43)

Quotes – "Man Serves The
Interests Of No Creature But
Himself"
https://www.shmoop.com > quotes
(44)

Dear Digger Doug
http://www.discoverymagazine.co
m/digger/d011dd.html

(45)

BOWLINGUAL
From Wikipedia, The Free Encyclopedia
http://en.Wikipedia.org/wiki/BowLingual
(46)

ENOADOET
"Korean Mobile carrier Offers Pet Translator Service"
Posted May 12, 2005 By Barb Dybwad
http://www.engadget.com/2005/05/12/korean-mobile--carrier-offers-pet-translator-service
(47)

"Emotion"
Wikipedia, The Free Encyclopedia
http://en.wikipedia.org/wiki/Emotion
(48)

"Do Animals Have Emotions?"
23 May 2007
By Marc Bekoff

Magazine Issue 2605
https://www.newscientist.com/article/
mg19426051.300
(49)

Quotes By Plutarch: "But For A
Mouthful Of Fle..."
https:/www.goodreads.com >
quotes
(50)

"What Is Temperament?" -
American Kennel Club
www.ak,.org > akctemptest >
what-l...
(51)

"Brain Mechanisms Of Drug
Reward And
Euphoria – PubMed"
https://pubmed.ncbi.nim.nih.gov...
(52)

"Pavlovian Conditioning –
Behavioral Psychology ..."–
Britannica

https://www.britannica.com > science
(53)

"Crying Cow Kneels In Front Of s\Slaughterhouse Workers Begging..."
https://www.dailymail.co.uk > c
(54)

Buddhist Quotes – "The Elated Vegan"
https://elated.co.za > buddist-quotes
(55)

"Animals Emotion Is Simple And Pure; Similarities Between Animal And..."
https://www.grandin.com > inc > ani
(56)

GLOBAL ANIMAL ALL ABOUT ANIMALS, FROM PETS TO WILD LIFE

"The Emotional Lives Of Cows"
By Joey Turner on July 8, 2011
"Cows behavior, emotions,
personality: cows have best
friends." – Global Animal
https://www./globalanimal.org/201
1/07/08/the-emotional-life-of-cows/
(57)

Lisa Gould: VCA Yorba Regional
Animal Hospital
https://vcahospitalscom > team >
lis
(58)

"Why And How To Read A Cow
Or Bull"
Hoard's Dairyman Mazazine
By Jack Albright
The author is professor ameritus
of animal science, Purdue
Universiy, West Lafayette,Ind.
https://nature.berkeley.edu/ucce5
0/
ag-labor/7article29.htm
(59)

"What Are The Impacts of Stress On pork Quality? - The Pig Site"
https://www.thepigsite.com. > articles
(60)

Quotes By Theophile Gautier "Who Can Believe There Is No Soul..."
https://www.goodreads.com > quotes
(61)

"The Inner World Of Farm Animals: Their Intellectual..."
By Amy Hatkoff
https://www.goodreads.com > show
(62)

"Moral Progress And Animal Welfare – ABC Religion & Ethics"
https://abc.net.au > religion
(63)

"Science, Medicine, And Animals – NCBI

Bookshelf – NIH"
https://www.ncbi.nlh.gov > pmc
(64)

Universal JMU
Liverpool John Moores University
Animal Emotions Research
"Research Shows That Animals
And Humans Experience The
Same Emotions"
http://www.ljmu.ac.uk/NewsCentr
e/67668.htm
(65)

"The Seattle Times:Living: Do
Animals Have Emotions? Well I'll
Be A Monkey's Uncle"
By Michael C. Bradury
Wednesday, November 1, 2006
http://www.seattletimes.nwsource.
com html/living/
2003333119_animals01,html
(66)

"Emotion In Animals"
From Wikipedia, The Free
Encyclopedia

http://en.wikapedia.org/wiki/Emotion_in_animals
(67)

"Science/Nature – Animals 'Are Moral Beings' – BBC NEWS"
http;//news.bbc.co.uk > science > bat…
(68)

"The Emotional Depth Of A Cow-Hannah Velten- Opinion-The Guardian"
https://www.theguardian.com > Opinion > Animal behavior
(69)

"Philosophical Ethics And The Improvement Of Farmed Animal Lives"
By PB Thompson – 2020 – Cited 3
https://www.academic.oup.com >article
(70)

"The Science Of Animal Emotions"

By Pierre Thomasand the ABCNEWS
Investigative Unit
November, 08, 2002
http://www.ABCNews.com
(71)

"Animal Emotions"
By Edward Willett
http://www.edwardwillett.com/Colum
ns/animalemotions.htm
(72)

"Loulis (chimpanzee)"
From Wikipedia, the free encyclopedia
http://en.wikipedia.org/wiki/Loulis
(73)

MAIL ONLINE
"Heifer So Lonely: How Cows
Have Best Friends And Get
Stressed When They Are
Separated"
By Daily Mail Reporter
Updated: 05:26 EST, 5 July 2011

https//www.dailymail.co.uk/scienc
etech/article-2011124s/Cows-best-
friends-s...
(74)

EVERYTHING2
"Animal Emotions"
Created By Inky
Tuesday, September 18, 2001 at
6:23:54
http://everything2.com/index.pl?
node_id=1160415
(75)

**"The Humane Society of
Greenwood – Cruelty
Prevention"**
http://www.gwdhumanesociety.or
g/cruelty.shtml
(76)

**"Two Bonobos Adopted Infants
Outside Their Group, Marking A
First For Great Apes"**
By Carolyn Wilke
March 18, 2021 At 12:00 P.M.

https://www.sciencenews.org...
(77)

"Do Animals Feel Grief"
-Psychology Today"
https://www.psychologytoday.com
>...
(78)

"Quotes – Laboratory Animals"
https.//www.animalmatters.org >...
(79)

" Can Animals Ever Feel Disgusted?" -
Quora
https://www.quora.com > Can anima...
(80)

Quote By Horace Man "Be
ashamed to die until you have..."
https://www.goodreads.com >
quotes
(81)

"Man is the cruelest of all animals"
Friedrich Nietzsche (1)

www.ingramcontent.com/pod-product-compliance
Lightning Source LLC
Chambersburg PA
CBHW062208280526
45788CB00001B/501